69 Th
To Do Whe...
Not Doing It

69 Things To Do When You're Not Doing It

THE IN-BETWEEN LOVERS HANDBOOK

CATHY HOPKINS
Illustrated by Gray Jolliffe

Fontana
An Imprint of HarperCollins*Publishers*

First published in Great Britain in 1991 by
Fontana, an imprint of HarperCollins Publishers,
77–85 Fulham Palace Road,
Hammersmith, London W6 8JB

9 8 7 6 5 4 3 2 1

A CIP record for this book is
available from the British Library

ISBN 0 207 17297 8

Printed and bound in Great Britain
by Scotprint Ltd, Musselburgh

CONTENTS

INTRODUCTION

Invariably in life, there are times when we all find our-selves 'between lovers' or simply just 'off sex'. These periods can last for hours, weeks, months, decades or if you really get hooked on it – lifetimes.

There are several ways to deal with the position:

1) Mope
2) Find another lover immediately
3) Find an interesting alternative

'People always analyse what makes them happy and go looking for God when their sex life is lousy,' my friend Serge declared on hearing of my intention to do this book. 'Call the book 69 sex substitutes.' 'How cynical,' I thought. Surely it couldn't be true that being alone is the only time our minds turn to alternative ways to fulfilment. Yet come to think of it, I was fourteen years old when I started looking for 'something more'. I was five foot nine inches and all the boys of my age were four foot ten inches and their favourite joke 'What's the weather like up there?' was wearing a bit thin. 'It's raining,' I spat returning to my new copy of *Mysticism in the East* with an extra section titled 'you are not your body.'

How to spot the norm

Many people do believe that to be in a relationship and have an active sex life is to be the norm, to be striven for at all times. This leaves single and celibate people conditioned into thinking that they must be missing out. But is sex really the pinnacle of experience? The high point of existence?

'Of course,' said Serge, 'but sex can even be mystical. It can transport you to other realms. It can be sublime, divine, ecstatic and you can feel a oneness with your partner I bet some of those mystics would die for. On the other hand it can be relaxing, exciting, challenging and gratifying on all levels. Sight, sound, taste and sensation.'

OK. Yes, that's good sex but what about the bad sex which can be emotionally traumatic, heart-breaking, unsatisfying, humiliating, boring, lonely, squelchy, sticky and can leave a damp spot on the kitchen table. It has its down side.

'Life's a bitch and then you die' friends often quote to each other when times are hard with the ups and downs of relationships and the slings and arrows of outrageous phone bills. Simple survival can sometimes be tough, what with the unavoidable comings and goings of an ever-changing world. Eating and sleeping so that we can work and working so that we can eat and sleep. Sometimes it can seem quite futile, with what we really want slipping further and further into the distant future. What's the point? Is sex the only break in the clouds?

It is said that change and a sense of humour are close to the heart of God. Could it be His ultimate joke that human beings – with all their aspirations to sophistication, higher intelligence and civilization – are at their happiest and most content naked with legs splayed, with grunting, heaving, groaning faces distorted with the pleasure of love-making? But then one only has to compare someone's face

on the brink of orgasm to the tranquil face in the painting by Rosetti, *The Divine Vision*, to consider that there may be different roads to ecstasy.

This book sets out to examine the various experiences people try in order to find fulfilment. Is it different for *everyone*? Is there a formula? Or is a bump, grind and a cuddle (no matter how prolonged or imaginatively delivered) the best on offer?

The most common sex substitutes are:

Chocolate	T.V.
Alcohol	Romantic fiction
Work	Smoking
Sleeping	Cars
Shopping	God-seeking
Drugs	Headaches
Babies	

And that's just for starters.

1

FOOD

1. EAT

> 'You know sourdough is very sexy.
> Whenever I don't have a girl I order a
> dozen a day'
>
> *Dustin Hoffman*

If you're ever wondering what to do when you're not
doing it, the unanimous cry of an enlightened species is
'feed your face'. Eat.

Unrequited? Suck on a sausage.
Angry? Attack a phallic symbol, bite a banana, slice
a salami, mutilate a marrow, crush a cucumber.
Frustrated? Swallow a phallic symbol. Any of the
above – whole.
Lonely? Surround yourself with food for company.
Jelly babies, dolly mixtures, gingerbread men, a trout
with its eye in.
Guilty? Nettle soup and three Hail Marys.
Horny? Meat and two veg. Fresh figs.

Foods to avoid: aphrodisiacs like oysters and rhino-horn juice and, of course, pineapple rings as there's no one to play hoopla with. And cottage cheese. No flavour, like kissing your sister.

Food. Most people's number one sex substitute. Food is great, it doesn't answer back. Doesn't judge or reject you. You'll never see a piece of pie backing off the plate saying, 'Oh no, not you, you've got bad breath' or, 'I saw you in that Thai place last night and you think you can come here and start where you left off'. No, you can indulge, experiment and try so many sensations. Food is impartial.

It satisfies, and if you can't get what you want in a relation-ship and you're feeling deprived, you can make up for it by eating the naughtiest and grossest bit of nosh you can lay your hands on. And when you've had enough you don't have to send it a 'Dear John' letter.

My friend Jenny (who's read lots of books, so she must know what she's talking about) explained it all to me. 'Man's first instincts are those of survival. Food, shel-ter, warmth, sex. Only when those needs are satisfied will he look further. Sometimes he never bothers at all and stays in those realms – the high point of his existence being a bonk and a biryani.'

I suppose that makes sense. I mean who cares about the ecstacy of art and opera if you're cold and hungry. Certain needs do have to be attended to. People do eat to survive, but they also eat to swallow anger, misery, bore-dom, repression, they eat as a substitute, as an avoidance, out of guilt, fear, dissatisfaction. But then eating can also be turned into an art, a creative venture with room for experimentation, careful selection of ingredients, recipes, the company with whom to share it. Some people dribble over erotica, others drool over recipe books.

There are so many comparisons – fast food, fast sex; instant food, instant sex (all over in five minutes and that's doing it twice for some people). Then there are the well prepared, the experts: food or sex is lingered over, sav-oured and appreciated to the last morsel.

What's most interesting, though, is what you can learn about people from the way they eat. Back in the eighteenth century Charles Lamb said, 'I hate a man who swallows food affecting not to know what he is eating. I suspect his taste in higher matters.' Indeed! I've been watching people for many years now, and as with sex you have to find a compatible partner, so with food.

Draw your own conclusions from the following:

Gobblers:	Ram it in. Don't chew and want immediate gratification.
Pickers:	Dissect the food. Examine it. Toy with it and leave most of it.
Sloshers:	Gloop it all together in a big lump.
Players:	Make their food into houses, faces, patterns.
Sprayers:	Spray food as they eat and talk with their mouths full letting you see the whole process of mastication.
Fussy Eaters:	Have to know where it's been, where it grew, how it was cooked. Organic? Preservatives?
The Indifferent:	Not interested. Whether it's the Roux brothers or McDonalds, they wouldn't know the difference.
The Gourmands:	Love it. Eat with pleasure.
Droolers:	Get it all over their faces and dribble.
Savers:	Keep the most succulent bit till last.
The Thorough Eater:	Chews each mouthful fifty times and leaves no trace on the plate.
Restrained:	Would like to let rip but can't for fear of getting fat, so make you feel guilty as you tuck in.
Gourmets:	Wouldn't be seen dead eating anything mediocre. No white bread (but croissants) no instant coffee (but imported Brazilian). Only the best, designer packaged and labelled.

Anyway, once fed and wined, what next?

Not sex. Good sex should always come before eating.

Dining dulls the senses and anyway who wants to make love on a full stomach? Many a couple has blown what could have been an intimate love-session because of a large curry.

Of course, this book is about sex-substitutes, but let's have a look at sex, even if it's just to see exactly what it is we're missing.

2

SEX

2. ZEN AND THE ART OF SELF-MAINTENANCE

> *'You are the greatest lover I have ever known.'*
> *'Well, I do practise a lot on my own.'*
> Woody Allen

Masturbation is: More than four shakes.
Sex with someone you love.
A way of meeting a better class of person.
Never having to say sorry.

The Pros: You can't catch anything you haven't already got.

Pros for him: You don't have to take your hand out to dinner to talk over its problems.
You don't have to send your hand thank-you notes and flowers.

You don't have to ask 'How was it for you?'.

Pros for her: You don't have to fake to please him.
You can take as long as you like.
You know exactly where the buttons are.
You don't have to look your best.

D.I.Y. tools for being handy about the house

a) A vibrator (but make sure it doesn't chip your teeth).
b) An inflatable love sheep (available at all good chemists).

> *Mary had a little sheep*
> *She took it into bed to sleep*
> *Alas! That sheep it was a ram*
> *Now Mary has a little lamb.*

New uses for everyday objects

a) The washing machine on spin (do sit *on* it, not *in* it, although that may be a memorable experience of a kind).
b) Candles (for the religious single, as you can use them for playing hymns. Do make sure they're not lit).
c) Assorted vegetables (not pickled unless you like being a sour puss).

3. ROMANTIC AND SEXUAL FANTASY

According to recent research in the States, more and more couples are favouring the 'doggie' position as opposed to the 'missionary' position. This is so participants can watch TV at the same time. (Though according to another survey, one third of women prefer reading in bed, this clearly requires yet another position. . .)

Most people's expectations about sex come from the myths derived from popular fiction, but it seems – when looking at various excerpts – that the fantasies vary slightly according to gender. . .

Hers: 'The magnetic quality of his merciless gaze burnt into her trembling heart. His proximity was unbearable. 'Come to me,' he whispered. Though she longed to be crushed by his magnificent being, she tried to murmur her resistance. He drew her towards him, only acknowledging her desire, her lips parted in anticipation as she lost herself in all-pervading sweetness of his wild and masterful embrace.' [And so on.]

His: 'Her eyes sparkled as she caught sight of the bulge in his uniform trousers. 'God, you're big,' she shuddered as she unfastened her 36 double D-cup bra with the other hand. She squealed with delight as he shoved his enormous pulsating ******* in her juicy ****. Then she came and he went home.'

In Short:

Hers: Tremble, sigh, hold back, resist, surrender.
His: Thrust, squeal, come, go.

But just what are we missing when in-between lovers?

People's attitudes to sex can vary enormously. Some, like Caesar (in days gone by), are all for it. 'I came, I saw, I bonked 'er' (in that order?). And then there's his wife who remarked after him, 'He came, I'm sore, I'm conquered.' Other attitudes can be found in the following quotes.

a) 'If treated properly, sex can be the most gorgeous thing in the world.'   *Elizabeth Taylor*

b) 'Conventional intercourse is like squeezing jam into a doughnut.'   *Germaine Greer*

c) 'You know the worst thing about oral sex? The view.'
                                                Maureen Lipman

d) 'I'd rather have a guy take me to a football match and have a drink afterwards than go to bed with someone.'
                                                    Samantha Fox

e) 'The most fun I've ever had without laughing.'
                                                    Woody Allen

f) '2½ minutes of squelching.'   *Johnny Rotten*

g) 'The pleasure is momentary, the position ridiculous and the expense damnable.'   *Lord Chesterfield*

h) 'I'd rather have a cup of tea and a good conversation.'
                                                    Boy George

It takes all sorts.

4. THE MOVIES

Pure escapism, whether you are disillusioned with love, or not. Have you ever seen the reality of sex and 'in-between' relationships in a movie amidst the dappled love scenes enacted by perfect bodies in perfect synch with each other? Well, yes, quite often but only through the subjective view of the director.

Try applying real life to the movies:

If in *Last Tango in Paris* Marlon had run out of butter.

If in *9½ Weeks* Kim couldn't join in the fun because of cystitis.

If James Bond couldn't rise to the occasion at all, the stress of his job finally affecting his performance.

If in *Pretty Woman* the heroine, instead of lying content and smug after the love scene, was left clawing the walls with frustration and the hero was labelled a lousy lover even after he'd tried his usual formula for success.

If Emmanuelle found she'd become frigid and couldn't figure out why it was. Her childhood? Her first sexual disasters? (Still, many are cold but few are frozen.)

Lousy sex for whatever reason is taboo on the big screen and can leave audiences with a lot to live up to. When the reality doesn't match the movie, people can feel let down and they imagine that everyone else's love life is rampant and much better than their own.

Everywhere you look, it's sex and more sex. Are you getting your quota? Do this or that questionnaire to find out. Are you doing it imaginatively? Karmasutracally? Happy, cosy couples represent what you should aspire to if you're not to be considered 'a bit odd' or incapable of sustaining a relationship. No doubt sex does have a lot to offer: affection, companionship, sensuality . . . but the biggest myth revolving around sex is the one that says someone is going to make you happy. Completely and utterly.

No one's perfect. The only person who can make you happy is yourself – so: enjoy the movies, just don't believe the schmalz.

Of course there are all sorts of movies to see, not just romantic ones. But these days they always seem to stick a sex-scene in there somewhere – whether it's in the sensual evening glow of the local looney bin or out on the lonesome prairie. And what do you know? It's lovely Lolita and her perfect silicone pair riding into the sunset.

3

THE JOY OF·BEING SINGLE

5. TREAT YOURSELF

B eing in a relationship can be a way to enjoy those good
things of life we might not otherwise allow ourselves.
You cook decent food if there are two of you, or buy
good champagne to make an occasion more special. Some
people hold back from treating themselves when alone, it
may seem selfish or indulgent, but having a lover to spoil
gives them permission to join in. Single needn't mean being
deprived or excluded from anything. To hell with guilt –
indulge, and forget the usual moan lines.

Moan	Alternative
I'm tired of being the spare one at dinner parties	So take someone of your own sex or organize your own single's only dinner
No one buys me flowers any more	Buy your own and buy a friend some while you're at it

There's no one to go to the movies or theatre with	Why miss out? Go on your own or join an agency. They're not all dating agencies, some are for companions
I miss being touched	Book a massage, it can be therapeutic and comforting
I miss the little treats	Create them yourself. Book tea for two at the Ritz. Buy fresh croissants and have friends for breakfast
I've nothing to do in my spare time	Find a hobby. There's no need to be bored. Only boring people get bored

Life is what you make it.

6. EXPLORE NEW EXPERIENCES

> 'You should make a point of trying every experience once, except incest or folk-dancing.'
>
> *Anon*

One of the joys of being single is the freedom to enjoy new experiences without criticism or query. Many a relationship breaks down because people want their partners

to satisfy and stimulate them on all levels, sex can then be the biggest barrier of all when it stops you seeking any other fulfilment or adventure for fear of upsetting or invalidating the relationship. People have different needs, different tastes, and if you're single you can experiment with them, you don't have to put all your legs in one basket.

There are all sorts of thrills to be sought: why not try sky diving, nuclear physics, ju-jitsu? (See Chapter 11 for more hobbies.)

7. GET A POSITIVE ATTITUDE

> *'I belong to Bridegrooms Anonymous.*
> *Whenever I feel like getting married, they*
> *send over a lady in a housecoat and curlers*
> *to scream at me and burn the toast.'*
> Dick Martin

Attitude is very important, so look at the pros of being single not the woes.

It's a strange phenomenon, but as a young child you have to share a room with brothers and sisters, then you reach a certain age and you are considered too grown-up to share. Then promotion! Perks! A room of your own. You get to use the bathroom in privacy. Bliss. You can read late at night, play music loud, plaster the walls with revolting posters.

Then, as years go by you may fall in love. You may decide to live with the one you love and suddenly it's a demotion in a *big* way. Suddenly you have to share not only a room again, but also a bed – not to mention wardrobe space and possibly even the bath!

Now, a kingsize jacuzzi is a possibility but not found in your average two up, two down. Take the average bath: avocado green, and not exactly beckoning with a promise of secret delight. Fine for two splashing toddlers but two oversized lilywhite adults? Doctor C in *The Sensuous Couple* says, 'No sensuous couple can claim to have a full repertoire of sexual technique until they make full use of the bath and the shower.' It's kind of hard to feel sensual with your bosom scalded on the taps, a foot in the toilet bowl and him with a bollock in the soap dish. And Lord knows where the soap is! All this in the name of sex and sensuality. It has a price.

The Pros of Being Single

You know where the soap's been.

You get to use the TV remote control.

You never wake up shivering to find he/she's got the whole duvet wrapped snugly round him/her.

You can read *Hello* magazine without being accused of being superficial.

You can use the bathroom with the door open.

You can use your glow-in-the-dark vibrator in the dining-room.

You can walk around naked without having to hold your stomach in.

You can watch 'Neighbours' and 'Dallas' without having

THINGS YOU CAN DO WHEN YOU'RE ALL ON YOUR OWN:

You can have three boxes of chocolates and a bottle of Baileys all to yourself.

You can make yourself ill without some busybody trying to give you the kiss of life.

to defend your IQ, or the football with your lager lout buddies.

You can have ice-cream for breakfast and custard and jam for dinner.

Basically you can do what you want.

8. FIND A PURPOSE TO GET OUT OF BED IN THE MORNING

Being in love can certainly put a spark into life, but if it's not on the cards at the moment find a campaign or a purpose you can pour your energy into and which can put new life into you and make you feel a part of it all.

Avoid the following hopeless causes:

a) Petitioning to get delivery men to give a definite time other than 'sometime Wednesday'.

b) Demanding more ladies' loos in English theatres. (The hopelessness of this cause is illustrated by this apocryphal, but seminal tale: a man was walking in a park and he sees another man making love to what seems to be an inanimate woman. He goes racing off to the park-keeper. 'Quick, there's a man over there making love to a dead body.' The park-keeper goes to see, returning moments later. 'She's not dead, sir, she's English.' In other words, the universal view is that not only do English women not bonk, they don't pee either – hence one loo to each theatre.)

Causes that might be fun

a) Putting on a show. It always worked in those early Judy Garland/Mickey Rooney movies.

b) Putting on another show. (Well, it worked for Judy Garland. . .)

c) Not putting on another show. (It worked for Anthony Newley.)

9. FIND SOMETHING OR SOMEONE TO LOVE

> *'Odd things animals. All dogs look up to you. All cats look down to you. Only a pig looks at you as an equal.'*
> *Winston Churchill*

We need to give love as well as get love to feel complete, so adopt a granny, buy a cat, a fish or a bird (but perhaps not all at the same time).

Pets can be wonderful company, they don't try to give you advice, they never try to borrow money, they're always so pleased to see you and they have no in-laws.

Hedgehogs: Can be a bit prickly sometimes. (According to the evening news, a Portsmouth man believed he'd found the way to talk to hedgehogs, although he didn't know the meaning of what he was saying to them.)

Parrots: 'There are limits to the conversation one can have with a parrot.'

Peter Ustinov

Dolphins: Perhaps a bit unrealistic as a household pet, as you need an extremely large pool or private bit of ocean to keep one in. But these creatures are apparently remarkable company and intelligent enough to have trained humans to stand on the poolside and throw them fish. The same goes for cats and dogs, in fact most pets have you running round after them as an unpaid slave.

Lobsters:
Ernie: What's that you've got there?
Eric: A lobster.
Ernie: A lobster? Are you taking it home for tea?
Eric: No, it's had its tea, now I'm taking it to the pictures.

Morecambe and Wise

Dogs:
You'll never find a more loyal friend and enthusiastic companion.
'Every day the dog and I, we go for a tramp in the woods. And he loves it! Mind you, the tramp is getting a bit fed up!'

Jerry Dennis

Cats:
The trouble with cats is that they believe you belong to them, not only do they expect you to feed them but also to entertain them – and often at 4am in the morning when you're trying to get some sleep. With a cat for company, you need never miss your ex-lover at all.

4

FRIENDS AND FAMILY

10. REDISCOVER YOUR FRIENDS

> *'Friends are God's apology for relations'*
> *Hugh Kingsmill*

Mary Catherwood remarked that 'two may talk together under the same roof for many years, yet never really meet, but two others at first speech are old friends.' Value these people. When you're down and out and times are low, who can you turn to? After a period in a relationship, it's quite sad sometimes to see how friends are neglected as couples withdraw into an exclusive cocoon. Sometimes you literally have to win friends and their trust back. Often in the first flush of new love, you forget the single friend and movie companion. Then romance crumbles, and the deserted friend is expected to pick up where you left off. Friends must never be regarded as sex-substitutes like this as they often outlast lovers, who come and go. Friends are the ones who know all about you and still like you. If you go through a strange patch, they don't believe it's permanent.

Rules for friends

a) If you want a friend, be a friend.
b) Be there for them as they are for you. As Bing Crosby said about Bob Hope, 'There's nothing I wouldn't do for Hope and there's nothing he wouldn't do for me. We've spent our lives doing nothing for each other.'
c) Don't just share the bad times with them or dump on them.
d) Value them and be prepared to discuss misunderstandings.
e) Don't lose your Christmas list, you might forget who your friends are.

Rules for enemies

a) We should forgive our enemies, but only after they've been shot.

11. TURN TO YOUR FAMILY

She: 'One more word and I go back to Mother.'
He: 'Taxi!'

SPOT THE FRIEND:
(a)
You look simply fantastic!
(b)
Yergh! You're got a bogey!

5

EXERCISE, DANCE AND BALLGAMES

12. GO JOGGING

A lot of people go jogging. But have you ever seen one of them looking like they're enjoying it? A happy jogger? I think they run to punish themselves for some deep, dark guilty secret. A bit of self-torture makes up for the dead body in the cellar.

It is said that at a certain level of exercise you produce a chemical that gives a real 'high'. It's interesting that in severe pain you also produce a chemical to numb the pain and to soothe the shock. Sounds like the same chemical to me.

Don't let me put you off, though. One man's treat is another man's nightmare (and most forms of exercise are mine). The thing is though, if you don't do any all sorts of horrible things sneak up on you:

apathy	stress
tension	fat
depression	cellulite
flab	the builder's bum cheeks. . .

'... Oberon what visions have I seen, methinks I was confronted by an ass.' A great lily-white pimply one at that.

But the truly, truly wonderful thing about exercise is that when it's over, and you are full of righteousness and pride, you can make your way to the nearest restaurant. Still, in the long run, exercise isn't a bad idea, but a short run is enough for most of us.

Take your pick from the following:

13. AEROBICS

A killer, you've got to be fit even to think about it.

14. ACROBATICS

You'll need to borrow a friend's biplane.

15. ALL-IN-WRESTLING

Good if you're particularly missing that intimate body contact.

16. BALL-GAMES

Cricket, football, badminton, squash, tennis, table-tennis, these are great if you've got pent-up anger. Focus it all on the ball – and whack it.

In the States they play baseball. I once asked my friend Teddy Tannenbaum just what *was* the appeal of baseball. This is what he wrote: 'As a ballplayer once said after hitting a ball four hundred feet along a sweet upward arc, "Man, that feels better than sex and almost as good as eatin' watermelon".

'Despite Mr George Bernard Shaw's remark that the only advantage baseball had over cricket was that "it was over sooner" you will find that the game rewards the patient observer and he/she whose senses have been made subtle.

'You see, there's no guilt in baseball. And it's never boring, which makes it like sex. Making love is like hitting a baseball, you just got to relax and concentrate.'

Anne Savoy (from the movie *Bull Durham*)

'All of which may never answer the age-old question of which came first: sex or baseball? But ask any guy who's tried his hand at both games. He'll remember his first sexual encounter, sure, but he'll remember in exquisite detail about that 400-foot home run with a couple of runners on base in the bottom of the ninth with the score tied and the game on the line. He'll remember who the

pitcher was, the count, the names of the runners on the base, the umpires, stadium, day, date, time, temperatures, wind velocity and what he had for breakfast before he came to the ballpark that morning.

'Even if he married that girl of his dreams, he goes to sleep at night replaying that home run day, what was, what is and what might have been if time and circumstance hadn't gotten in the way.'

Thanks, Teddy, now I understand. I guess the same could be applied to the other ball games, sex included: the movement is limited, and predictably someone always ends up on the floor covered with mud being kissed frantically.

17. CYCLING

Very dangerous but good for the bum.

18. CANOEING

Great fun until you lose your paddle.

19. SCUBA-DIVING

Better in the Tropics than off Wigan Pier.

20. DANCING

Ballroom dancing, ballet, boris dancing for Russians, folk dancing, belly dancing, Zulu dancing.

Egyptian dance

Why not try a more exotic type of exercise? In days gone by, dance was used by various cultures as a means to express emotion from sorrow to joy.

In ancient Egypt, the trance dance was particularly interesting. All the women at court would come together and dance it all away. Having seen it performed on stage, it is easy to see how therapeutic it must have been, the gestures being thoroughly despondent and ill-tempered, arms and head tossed this way and that in disdain and indifference until the pace builds, the movements becoming more rhythmic, passionate, aggressive and thrusting, flinging the limbs in an almost African and tribal manner into the last swirling throws of the dance.

What we take in the west is a gin and tonic and a valium. The old method was far more effective and you could drive afterwards.

Imagine the usual scenarios in city life, queues in the post office, delays on the underground. 'Life, an endless standing in line', as Mencken said. Instead of the more usual resigned sigh, tightening chest and jaw as we distract ourselves reading some banal poster on the wall, what if . . . down comes the post office manager or station master and lines everyone up for the trance dance. Housewives, stockbrokers, students, tourists, shoppers. . . It's fling to the left, then to the right, shake it out, throw it out, ayee, ayee (this dance is best when accompanied by a bit of mad

shouting). Roll the head. Flop down from the waist. Yowl and round in a circle we go.

But it's inconceivable, and certainly not British. So we bury our head deeper into our newspapers to avoid anyone's gaze and read the latest findings about stress in the Nineties. A good shakedown would work wonders I reckon, at the very least it would get our insides going, pump blood and air to the lungs.

21. HORSERIDING

More popular with girls than boys strangely enough. Unless there's money in it.

22. JUDO

Ideal for the next time you want to chuck someone.

23. SKATING

A whole new crowd of people to go round with.

24. SWIMMING

Great exercise, and when you reach France you can have coffee and croissants.

25. ROWING

Builds up arm and shoulder muscles, useful in the pub situation.

26. WEIGHT-TRAINING

But if you're a girl, don't do it please.

27. WIND-SURFING

Doing it standing up will never seem the same again.

28. WINTER SPORTS

Toboganning, skiing – though be careful not to break a leg, especially one of yours.

6

THE WORK EXPERIENCE

29. CAREER

A career can work two ways as a sex substitute:

Negative

It can be used as an avoidance, an excuse for not having a social or sex life. Meetings, deadlines, planning, all filling in time conveniently so one never has to face the fact that one is shy or inept when it comes to relationships. In which case, it's really a cop-out.

Positive

It can provide someone with all the stimulation and fulfilment missed by submergence in a love affair.

There are so many stories about people blossoming after splitting up from a partner. Sometimes the choice is sink or swim and you are literally thrown on your own resources. Although relationships do have much to offer on many levels, mainly the horizontal, they can also be used as an excuse not to develop one's real potential. Some people look back on break-ups as the best thing that ever

happened to them. A good old plummet into the depths – though murky and dark at the time – can bring forth all sorts of treasure. It's a way you can discover a great deal about yourself.

Lao Tzu said, 'The longest journey begins with the first step.' True. Unless, of course, the step is backwards or sideways.

It's never too late to start again – a new course, or a new job. While in a relationship, if bored and unfulfilled at work, sex can be used as a release, an escape and sometimes too much can be demanded of it. If job satisfaction is forthcoming, sex can be put in perspective. Life is too short to be dissatisfied in an area as time-consuming as work. So if you *are* dissatisfied, start putting out feelers, knocking on different doors, checking out possibilities.

But if you lack the confidence or fear the risk of change, the next chapter's for you.

7

THE NEW AGE

30. THERAPY

> Q 'How many therapists does it take to change a light bulb?'
> A 'One, and that is only if the light bulb wants to change.'

Some people want to know why they're 'in-between' lovers and have been for years. Some people aren't happy with the situation and want to know how and why it came about. Therapists can give a variety of explanations and advice:

a) You created the situation. Choice not chance determines destiny. Beliefs and attitudes learnt early on can shape and influence our decisions, so if you get in a mess, you're the only one who can get out of it.
b) Maybe you can't control events, but you can control your response and reaction. You haven't had a lover in years, you can be miserable or delighted about it.

c) Before change comes decay, then renewal. The darkest hour before dawn theory.

d) Let go and flow with the current of life. What you resist, persists.

e) Hold on. Fight. Don't give in.

f) Your elder brother tried to kill you when he was two and a half. You haven't felt safe since and won't trust anyone.

g) You had a bad birth experience and keep creating what's familiar.

h) You're ugly and smelly.

Confused? I'm not surprised. It's no wonder so many people are allergic to psychotherapy and bury their heads.

Annie: Oh, you see an analyst.
Woody: Yeah, just for fifteen years.
Annie: Fifteen years?
Woody: Yeah, I'm going to give him one more year then
I'm going to Lourdes.

Woody Allen

31. TAKE THE LEAP
DO A WEEKEND WORKSHOP

The various workshops on offer claim to help people
acquire different skills in different areas from communi-
cation to sexual freedom, assertiveness and independence.
Some are excellent, some are beyond stupid, but at the very
least they provide a chance for people to come together,
discover that they're not alone in their particular hangups
and confusions and they learn to laugh at them. Before
embarking on such a treatment, though, it's advisable to
learn some of the 'jargon':

New Age Speak	*Old Age Translation*
Don't be a victim	Chin up
I'm discovering my self-worth	The fees are going up 30 per cent
I've discovered my female side	I cry at sad movies
I've discovered my male side	I can be a bossy bugger

I'm on a learning curve	I don't know what the fxxx I'm doing
It was a valuable lesson	I totally cocked up and will never do 'that' again
Re-balancing	Having a lie down
Centreing	Having a lie down
Meditating	Having a lie down

I'm not into money or material possessions	Get the bill, will you? And can I sleep at your place?
Just go with the flow	My flow. Just don't argue and everything'll be OK.

32. THE HOLISTIC APPROACH

> *'My soul is crushed, my spirit sore, I do not like me anymore.'*
> *Dorothy Parker*

Once upon a time it was tea and sympathy from friends and family if you were ill, lonely, down, in-between lovers, frustrated or unhappy. But with the New Age dawning comes a time of change, growth, renewal and rebirth. All these things, but no sympathy. You might not want advice, therapy, explanations or solutions but sure enough some enlightened soul will set you straight. This is the treatment you're likely to get:

1) Why have you made yourself ill?
2) I didn't. There was a bug going round the office.
1) Yes, but you let it in. Probably because you've been hiding in your work, it's your body's way of telling you to slow down and face the facts.
2) But, but. . .
1) Or you're holding back your anger, it's got trapped and is coming out physically. Have you got a sore throat?

2) Yes. . .
1) [gleefully] I knew it. Repression, trapped. I told you
   so.
2) I don't suppose there's any chance of a honey and
   lemon.
1) What! No! Gargle wild nettles, that's what you need.
   Anyway I'm off now to my crystal healing with the
   ancient Red Indians of Stanmore. . .

Just what you need when you're ill. Guilt plus the responsi-
bility of having brought it on yourself in the first place.
Whatever happened to Lucozade and a bunch of daffs?

They'll all be there at the end round your coffin saying
that this was nature's way of telling you to take a break,
and just what were you trying to escape in adopting this

rather extreme avoidance tactic? Death. The ultimate cop-out.

A similar thing happened recently to Jenny. She was laid up with bad knees. The calls came. 'It means you don't want to go forward.' Oh thanks. 'Can you bend it? No? It means you're stubborn and obviously unbendable, ha, ha!' In the meantime she had three kids to feed, no shopping in, just a fridge full of mouth-watering explanations, fresh from the last workshop gang.

The really professional holistic practitioners aren't so callous, but they will go into your history to determine the root causes of physical and emotional symptoms. If you have been hurt by love or stressed by separation some of these treatments are very soothing, others quite painful. See what you fancy from the below:

33. ACUPUNCTURE

In the old days this was called voodoo and you used to stick needles into a doll. These days you just stick them straight into the person. If you want, you can go back to the old method, get a doll and treat your friends or ex-lovers from a distance.

34. AROMATHERAPY

Closest thing to heaven.

35. REFLEXOLOGY

Fun with feet.

36. OSTEOPATHY

For a cracking good time.

37. SWEDISH MASSAGE

For when you need to be kneaded.

38. IRIDOLOGY

This is for when you miss someone looking deep into your eyes. Except rather than telling you how beautiful you are, they may tell you your liver's packed up.

These treatments are useful for people who believe mind, body and emotions are linked, and who want to get on with life feeling positive and healthy. Other people choose a totally different way. One that promises an easier route. The road to escape.

8

DRUGS, DRINK AND DEBAUCHERY

39. DRINK

> 'Three Highballs and I think I'm St
> Francis of Assisi'
> *Dorothy Parker*

Of course there are days best survived with the help of as
many Tequila slammers as you can down. And one more.

Days when you come home to find:

Your lover in bed a) with one of your parents
b) with one of your friends
c) with one of your pets
d) wearing your clothes

The cat's been sick in the hall. The burglars have
been. The plumber hasn't. And it's the coldest winter
since 1803.

You've lost your job. You've found dry-rot. Your
holiday's been cancelled. You've got a date and
you've broken out in herpes.

Sounds like one hell of a day. No wonder you're hitting the booze
Yeah—and then to cap it all my stupid boyfriend went and drowned in the bath

You get the idea: all those glorious moments that are all part of life's rich tapestry, days when the immortal words of Scarlett O'Hara make a lot of sense, 'I can't think about this today. I'll go mad if I do. I'll think about it tomorrow! Hand me a beer.'

Otherwise as far as drink goes, watch your units, watch your driving and don't become too dependent on it. Drink in excess dries your skin, rots your liver, puts bags under your eyes, causes headaches and impotence. Drink can be the urination of you. And we say 'good health' as we down another.

Pick a cocktail according to mood:

Suicidal	Have a Zombie Special or a Kamakaze
Depressed	Cheer up on a Savoy Corpse Raiser or a Gloomraiser
Randy	A Slow Screw Up Against The Wall (seven of them) or a Dot's Hot Spot, experiment with a Spinster's Surprise or a Green-eyed Monster
Naughty	Have a Fallen Angel, a Devil's Kiss or a Sinful Sadie
Nostalgic	Remember your ex with a Tangy Highball, a Little Lowball, a Velvet Hammer, a Yellow Finger or a Death by Cobblers
Nasty	Swallow a Rabbit's Revenge
Frustrated	Chill out on a Fire Extinguisher

And finally, if you feel like making a new start, what else but a Virgin Between the Sheets?

If, however, you are feeling in need of total obliteration and none of the above appeals, try mixing them all together.

CHLOÉ'S HANGOVER REMEDY:

You will need to organize your hangover cure before you start.

40. DRUGS

> 'Reality is just a crutch for people who can't cope with drugs'
> *Robin Williams*

One lady I read about liked to take LSD. Again and again she experienced 'The Secret of Life' with absolute clarity. The trouble was, she could never remember what it was the next day. Finally she remembered, while under the drug's influence, to write it down. The next day she eagerly looked to see what she had written. There it was, the secret of life, 'If I stand on my tiptoes I can reach the ceiling.' So much for drug insight.

Most mind-expanding drugs are downers, even the uppers. The escape is temporary and I've never seen anyone get the better of them. As Tallulah Bankhead wisely said, 'Cocaine isn't habit forming. I should know, I've been using it for years.'

There was a young fellow named Bill
Who took a mind-blowing pill
His entrails corroded
His belly exploded
And his balls were found in Brazil.

These tend to be the general effects:

Acid:	Watch Grandma turn into Helen of Troy, then the Wicked Witch from the Wizard of Oz.
Valium:	Life becomes a 3-D Leonard Cohen album.
Speed:	Get up at 10.20. Take speed. By 10.30 you will have done the ironing, retiled the bathroom and still be raring to go. . .
Marijuana:	'Marijuana makes you sensitive. Courtesy usually has a great deal to do with being sensitive. Unfortunately marijuana makes you the kind of sensitive where you insist on everyone listening to the drum solo in Iron Butterfly's "In-a-gadda-vidde" 50 to 60 times at 78rpm.' *P. J. O'Rourke*

Heroin: Avoid all needle drugs, you may be a dope but you're not worth shooting.

Cocaine: 'God's way of saying you're making too much money.' *Robin Williams*

Glue: ½ aspirin, ½ glue, great if you've got a splitting headache, and want a bigger one.

And if none of the above appeal, for something really different read on.

9

THE WEIRD AND WHACKY

41. MEDIUMS

Psychic practitioners have never had it so good. Some people need to be told by some higher power that they are basically OK, going the right way and love is just around the corner, and who better to tell them than the psychic practitioner?

> 'Stop stranger there as you go by
> As you are now, so once was I
> As I am now, so you shall be
> So be prepared to follow me.'
>> *Gravestone Engraving*

To which someone had added:

> 'To follow you I'd be content
> If only I knew which way you went.'

Perhaps insight and advice does lie with those who have passed on, but why should these 'spirits in the beyond' be able to help unless they're Claire Rayner types. Perhaps all the Aunty Bettys, Uncle Harrys and Grandma Lizzies who frequent seances in spirit and speak through mediums keep in touch in the hope that we might be able to help them.

Medium: 'Anyone here called Kevin, someone coming through for Kevin. It's Uncle Harry, I woke up last Thursday with no body, no, no *body*. I'm up here floating around. Haven't got a clue where I am. It's put a whole new meaning on being legless.'

It is interesting that the type of spirits that come through seem to vary from the sublime to the ridiculous. It's either

Doris or Plato, Fred or Big Chief Umpah, Red Indian warrior. How do we know that the 'grander' spooks are who they say they are and not some young prankster bogies having a laugh like teenage schoolkids? 'Let's contact some guy back on Earth and tell him it's Socrates with a message of great importance for the human race.'

42. CLAIRVOYANTS

Some will look into the future, some into the past.

He: You look familiar. Maybe we met in some previous life.

She: Gosh, how romantic. Like Antony and Cleopatra?

He: Or my mother, or my wife.

She: Or your lover.

He: Nope! I've got it, you were my pet frog.

A clairvoyant I met once told me she gets three to four women a week going to her believing that they were Cleopatra. She recalled one who had got particularly upset when told she'd only been a poor lonely washerwoman. She declared the clairvoyant a phoney and stormed out. (I could have easily told that woman she wasn't Cleopatra. I mean, how could she have been, when I was?)

Whatever you were, you've still got to pay the phone bills now. Wise men say our incarnations are progressive, so this must be the best so far. In that case do you really want to know about the others? Some people do find it inspiring to imagine that once they were someone special – a prince, a samuri, Marilyn Monroe.

In the meantime this life ticks on. If it's true that what we were has made us what we are, then surely what we're doing now is creating the future. Also if you keep looking backwards, chances are you'll walk into something.

43. ASTROLOGY

Given the time and date of your birth, a good astrologer can be deadly accurate. So you can always go along to see one of them to see if the stars predict a happier future, or a time of frustration.

> *'If you had been born two days later you would have been kind, generous and witty.'*
>
> *Hoest cartoon caption*

But what you may have to come to terms with is the fact that astrologically you've got the makings of an axe-wielding psychopath who's never going to get laid again. Nevertheless a visit to an astrologer can be very interesting – after all, imagine a whole hour or so spent talking about nothing but you. (But if they mention anything about seven-year cycles or Saturn and Pluto square to the Sun, plug your ears and make a run for it. There are times when ignorance is bliss.)

The In-Between Lovers Horoscope Guide

How the various signs may deal with the (just-elbowed) situation.

Aries	Panic. Get very drunk then plunge into the next chapter, person or project
Taurus	Eat
Gemini	Get out their little black book and find a replacement
Cancer	Cry and withdraw into their shell
Leo	Sulk, be dramatic and make sure they have lots of photos taken of them at their darkest hour for their portfolio
Virgo	Analyse what happened while clearing out any remains
Libra	Agonize about having made a decision (or gone along with one), then get stoned on grade A Columbain boogie dust
Scorpio	Seek revenge
Sagittarius	Shrug it off and buy a one-way ticket to Katmandu
Capricorn	Cross the ex-lover off their Christmas list and put it down to statistics
Aquarius	Was I having a relationship? And it's over? . . OK
Pisces	Will perfect the art of wistfulness, adopt tragic poses while writing heartwrenching poetry

Recommended 'in-between' lover activities:

Aries	Aries people love leaping off things, so anything involving: parachute jumping, deep-sea diving, hang gliding.

Taurus	A very sensual sign, you would miss being touched. Massage and general pampering from head to toe would keep you happy.
Gemini	Thrive on people and communication. Go to the theatre, exhibition openings, entertain.
Cancer	Need to feel safe. If not in a love affair turn attention to the home. A course in interior decorating and home improvement.
Leo	You like to be the centre of attention so go for the big time, enrol in a drama society. Become a performer.
Virgo	Psychotherapy, where you can confront, transform and metamorphasize to your heart's content.
Libra	Need romance, so travel to romantic destinations, like Paris and Venice.
Scorpio	Kung-fu, clay-pigeon shooting, archery, to channel the indignation of being single.
Sagittarius	Enjoy adventure, anything new and different: drag racing, ballooning, war games.
Capricorn	Happiest when building bricks in your career. Put your energy into achievements at work or night school.
Aquarius	Anything different, to satisfy your curious mind. (Quantum physics, brass rubbing, lassooing, tai-chi. . .)
Pisces	Write sonnets, sing ballads, paint and dance like Isadora Duncan (but leave off the neck scarf).

10

INTO THE MYSTIC

44. MEDITATION

One way of dealing with what to do when you're not
doing it is to transcend.

To be is to do	*Rousseau*
To do is to be	*Sartre*
Doo be doo be doo	*Sinatra*

To be a human 'being' instead of a human doing (driving,
walking, working) is the aim. To concentrate the mind to
a point where it is tranquil. It's a great theory until you
try it, then it goes something like this:

Thought 1:	OK. I'm feeling quite still and blank now.
Thought 2:	You can't be. You just thought that thought.
Thought 1:	What thought?
Thought 2:	The one about feeling blank. If you were really blank, you wouldn't think anything.
Thought 1:	OK. Let's try again.

MEDITATION:

My mind is blank - well sort of..
Why am I doing this
What should I wear?...
Dont forget Annie's party tonight
SHUT UP the lot of you!

Thought 3:	Oh, God, how many of us are there in here?
Thought 4:	Me.
Thought 5:	And Me.
Thought 6, 7, 8:	And us, and us.

It's not easy, why not just trying begging for help?

45. PRAYER

> 'If you talk to God you are praying. If God talks to you you have schizophrenia.'
>
> *Thomas Szasz*

Prayer is a great comfort to many people but I've always wondered which language to use. I mean:

a) What makes us assume He speaks our native tongue. He might only speak Swahili or Urdu.
b) If He does speak all languages, what kind of exchange system has He got? Or can He take 80 million calls all at the same time?
c) What do you pray to or at? And why do so many people direct their prayers to the ceiling?
d) Is He a he, or a she, or a bi or an it?
e) And just what do you say to such a being?
   'Er, excuse me your Royal Sir. I know you're busy watching everything, spinning planets, growing plants, changing seasons, breathing life into everyone, keeping

it all in balance and all, but could you just spare me a moment. But then, since you're omniscient, you know what I'm going to say anyway so maybe I shouldn't waste your time, but then you live in eternity which is timeless anyway. I'm afraid I'm not being very clear. Could you, of course you could, you're omnipotent. I

wasn't being derogatory. Maybe I shouldn't ask for anything because I guess you know best really. P.S. But could you let me have a few million, let there be peace and everyone be happy, and no lonely people, get to my goal weight and find the G-spot, that is if that's OK with you and doesn't interfere with your plans. Ah men, I mean, Amen.

It's a hive of bees once you start, so many mysteries, so many questions. Enough to act as a sex-substitute by taking your mind off it for at least fifteen minutes.

46. PHILOSOPHY

> 'What if everything is an illusion and nothing exists? In that case, I definitely overpaid for my carpet.'
> Woody Allen

Subjects to philosophize about:

a) Why we're here in the first place?
b) How do the men who drive the snow plough get to work in the morning?
c) Where have we come from?
d) What do you give a sick florist?
e) 'Chief amongst the mysteries of India is how the natives keep those little loin cloths up.'   Robert Benchley
f) Why do people long for eternity when they don't know what to do on the weekend?

g) Ghosts can walk through walls, how come they don't fall through the floor.
h) Where do all the lost socks go?

Philosophy can be mind boggling, as Macaulay said about Socrates, 'The more I read him, the less I wonder that they poisoned him'.

47. GOD SEEKING

> *'Almost all religions agree that God is fond of music, sometimes of dancing and always of processions.'*
> *Robert Morley*

Some people are seekers in this life. They want 'more', whether in or out of relationships. They search for something higher, the ideal, a God. But what do we really know about this power? It doesn't advertise on TV or put labels on its designs. . .

What we do know about God/god

a) He's a best selling author (the Bible)
b) Omnipresent, omnipotent, omniscient, omniomni.
c) Is one (unknown one what though?).
d) Might be three in one, God the Father, God the Son, God the Spirit.
e) Has a strange sense of humour, e.g. the human race – particularly insurance salesmen, wars, famines, ostriches.

Pros of having a God

Someone to talk to who doesn't answer back.

Someone to blame.

Someone who holds the supply of hope, promise and happiness (like a Santa Claus for adults).

Cons of having a God

Bigger than us.

Only moves in mysterious ways.

Omniscient, a know-it-all.

Omnipresent (no privacy, anywhere)

Omnipotent, better connected than the Godfather. If you can get in with him this can be a tremendous 'pro' for having a god. Problem is getting him on your side. (As Woody Allen said, 'How can I believe in God, when just last week I got my tongue caught in the roller of an electric typewriter.')

---

48. GET INTO RELIGION

Religion gives some people the foundation they seek, a lifestyle to follow and the promise of 'an answer'.

Christianity

> 'Deep down underneath it all, I have the heart of a small boy. I keep it in a jar on my desk.'   Robert Bloch

Christ said we must be like small children to enter the Kingdom of Heaven, innocent and gentle. Yet, as has been pointed out, no one ever made more trouble than 'gentle Jesus meek and mild'; the same goes for children. Half an hour alone in a room and you've got chaos.

Buddhism

The Buddha said:

a) All in life is temporary.
b) Suffering is a result of this.
c) Because we attach ourselves to these temporary things, we get upset when they end.
d) The answer is to find something not subject to change and attach yourself to that.

But what is constant, besides the fact that the phone always rings just as you've got into the bath?

Hinduism

Krishna took a similar view. He said that all this life is *maya* (meaning illusion). It's constantly changing and will be just as a passing dream when we awaken.

As W. C. Fields said, 'I dunno, it's a funny old world, so many questions, a man's lucky to get out of it alive.' In the meantime, while awaiting divine intervention, it may be simpler to stick to the simple life at home and find a hobby.

11

CHOOSING A HOBBY

> *There are two hobbies in Hollywood –*
> *jogging and helping newly-divorced*
> *friends move.*
>
> *Robert Wagner*

Of course there are hundreds of hobbies to choose from. Here are a few suggestions.

49. COLLECT ANTIQUES

Spend time browsing in markets and stalls, so you can buy back your grandmas old vases, the ones your mother threw out last spring.

50. READING

Books are an endless source of wonder, learning and insight into other lives and countries. And they're always handy as fly-swatters.

51. CARS

Cars are always worth spending time and care on as they often outlast lovers, and if they don't, their repayments will.

52. COOKING

So many recipes to experiment with these days. So many new books full of stirring advice. . .

53. KEEP A DIARY

As Mae West said, 'Keep a diary, one day it may keep you.'

54. FISHING

A relaxing, tranquil hobby for the stressed. (Except in the case of the fisherman who complained to his wife that he hadn't had a bite all day. So she bit him.)

55. GARDENING

Gardening is extremely rewarding, especially when you start to see what you've planted coming up. Try planting cabbages, carrots and razors, you get a lovely crop of coleslaw.

56. LEARN A NEW LANGUAGE

Mastering a new language not only gives you a new freedom when abroad, but also a sense of achievement. It can be difficult, though, because all the new words you have to learn aren't written in English.

57. MAGIC

Break the ice at dinner parties with a stunning set of magic tricks. Beware of losing your concentration, however, especially when doing 'a sawing a woman in half' illusion. One man Denis Norden spoke of did it, it almost proved fatal, but luckily the woman is now living contentedly in Scarborough. And Devon.

58. MUSIC

Take up an instrument, anyone can master a CD player, but an oboe is more challenging as well as an obvious phallic symbol.

59. NUDISM

Getting all your clothes off is a great feeling, whether around the house or in a field. (Not in the supermarket, though, unless you want tongues to wag.)

60. OPERA

This is when a woman finds she's got something terminal and instead of dying, sings with gusto at the top of her voice for two hours. If this is your cup of tea, then try opera. Personally I think it would be preferable without the singing.

61. POETRY

Reading or writing, although if you write it don't expect anyone to take you seriously until after you've died, preferably a long, debilitating illness, then you'll probably hit the bestseller list and become very rich.

62. PHOTOGRAPHY

Buy a camera, join a club, snap away, have hours of fun in the darkroom. And there could be money in it if you're in to doing weddings.

63. TRAVEL

Expensive, but a great way to spend a year or two. But remember if God had intended us to fly he'd have given us tickets.

64. TRAINSPOTTING

Well, someone's got to do it. All you need is a pencil and an anorak.

65. THEATRE

Fringe is best, try going on the stage and amuse your friends.

66. SHOPPING

According to Joan Rivers the only time a woman has a true orgasm is when she's out shopping. Every other time she's faking it. Sounds like the perfect 'in-between' lovers hobby, so get out there, girls!

67. COLONIC IRRIGATION

Big in America! Give one or receive one, it's certainly an effective way of clearing out the old rubbish.

12

THE SECRET OF HAPPINESS

> 'The search for happiness is one of the chief sources of unhappiness.'
>
> Eric Hoffer

68. LOOK FOR HAPPINESS

> 'When I was young, I used to think that wealth and power would bring me happiness. I was right.'
>
> Graham Wilson

According to a provincial newspaper, a nine-year-old girl was given a lesson on the value of wealth and stole the demonstration money. It's a lesson taken to heart at an early age. Money can get you what you want. There's no doubt that money does bring lots of freedom of choice, less strain over bills and so on, but it can be a bit of a con for a while. I'd be happy if I had a better bike, car, house, holiday, body and all that money can buy until oops! time's up and that elusive state with all the things you thought would make you happy haven't.

In an American survey on the most common words uttered at the time of death, they found that 'oh shit' were the most frequent. Is that 'oh shit, time's up and what have I done with it?', or, 'oh shit, I still haven't got my Merc?'. Apparently other common last words uttered by females were, 'Where's my bag?', perhaps in the belief that the myth continues on 'up there' and one only has to brandish an American Express card to whoever's on the gate to hear a benign, 'That'll do nicely', and you're in. Just for your information, other famous last words were:

'Either the wallpaper goes or I do.' *Oscar Wilde*
'They'll never hit us at this dist. . .' *General Custer*

To get back to wealth! I'm not knocking it, I agree whole-heartedly with Woody Allen that money is better than poverty if only for financial reasons, but some of the most miserable people I know are wealthy and the others are flat broke.

Thomas Szazz said, 'Happiness is an imaginary condition formerly attributed by adults to children and by children to adults.' It could also be added 'by the poor to the rich, the single to the married, the blonde to the brunette and vice versa'. Someone else has always got it, the other man's grass greener.

An essential key word in the happiness formula is appreciation – lose that and you can have it all, a great lover, money, family, career and it'll give you no joy. To know the price of everything and the value of nothing.

Dorothy Parker once said that the two most beautiful words in the English language are 'cheque enclosed'.

Joyce Grenfell had a less material value, 'Happiness is the sublime moment when you get out of your corsets at night'.

Happiness is often born of deprivation ended, a struggle relieved. A loo when you're bursting, a drink when you're thirsty, seeing a lover after being away, goals accomplished, circumstances survived. All these can bring about the wonderful state of appreciation.

> 'To be without some of the things you want is an indispensable part of happiness.'
>
> Bertrand Russell

So why not create a time of strain, then relieve yourself.

a) Invite fifty unsavoury houseguests round for a few days. Cook and clean for them, then send them away. Go for a long, fragrant bath while someone else clears up and prepares a banquet for you and someone you really like. (Jesus was the first to try this theory out. He invited beggars and tramps in off the street to a wedding feast and later he went and had supper with his real mates, twelve of them. Sadly, though, it turned out to be his last.)

b) Turn on the heating for a week. Take cold baths. Then turn it all back on.

c) Do the Cambridge diet for a week, then have a blow-out at the most elegant restaurant in town.

d) Have a celibate time 'in-between' lovers, meet someone new and go on to the next number.

69.

Well, this *is* the 'in-between lovers handbook'. . .

Ok, I've tried sex and I've tried celibacy. There's gotta be something else.